Terms and Conditions

Table Of Contents

Foreword

Being truly happy is an achievable state of mind. One only needs to be guided and the rest is up to the individual to put into practice. Being truly happy does not only have positive effects on the body but it also effects the condition of the mind.

Achieving Happiness

Dump Despair And Learn To Achieve True Happiness For You And Your Loved Ones

Chapter 1:

What Does True Happiness Really Mean

Synopsis

There are many scientific and natural therapy ways to achieve some level of happiness. With practice and conscious perseverance it is possible to achieve almost complete true happiness. Here are some insights as to how to make this possibility a reality.

The Start Point

Being a people person has the benefits of creating a happy and comfortable state of mind which in turn transcends into a happy reality. People who have various different relationships in their lives or are able to share their daily life cycles with others are often noted to be happy people.

Being a caring person also creates a level of happiness in an individual. The knowledge and satisfaction gained from being able to extend a helping hand is indeed gratifying.

Doing voluntary work or simply spending time with people in need of companionship can and usually bring great mental rewards.

Exercising regularly is also associated with a high degree of happiness. When the human body is running like a well tuned engine then all is well and this is clearly shown in the individual's demeanor and state of mind. Happy people are almost always healthy people; the state of the mind ensures this.

Having a hobby or goal that is fulfilling is also another way to focus on achieving happiness. Doing something on a daily basis that is not only enjoyable but also fulfilling brings about the general feeling of happiness and joy.

For some people being spiritually connected is being happy. Spiritual fulfillment help an individual to be one with both body and mind, and this is achieved then the surroundings have little or no negative impact on their lives.

Chapter 2:

Experience And Honor Your Feelings

Synopsis

Feelings are like an inner compass for any individual. In the quest to understanding one's feelings the individual is better equipped to handle whatever comes into their life's path. Being in touch and acknowledging one's feeling also allows for the individual to explore these feeling and thus become more aware of what brings him or her true happiness.

Recognize

However one must also be aware of the follies of just following one's feelings with the discerning intelligence of the mind. Sometimes following one's feelings can lead to less than desired circumstances and problems, thus feelings should be check before allowing it to be the dominant factor in executing things.

Here are some ways to experience and honor the individual's feeling without the detrimental effects if can or is likely to cause.

When the mind tells the body it is feeling something, the first thing to do, is to try to identify the said feeling and categorize it accordingly. In doing so, one can then discern if this feeling, if indulged will bring positive or negative results.

Once the feeling has been acknowledged then the process of understanding the reason for the feeling can begin. Only then should the feeling be indulged in or totally disregarded. Generally after an unbiased discerning exercise is done, the feeling if still strong, usually means that is it going to be fairly dominating in the individual's life.

Exercising a certain degree of validation of the said feeling is important. All too often people tend to disregard their feelings and emotions that are linked to the feeling and this can cause grave damage is left unchecked for too long.

Therefore it may be prudent to exercise indulgence to a certain degree in a particular feeling if the outcome is found to be non destructive and instead producing wonderfully positive results.

Chapter 3:

Put Together A Daily Ritual

Synopsis

Starting the day on a positive note usually means the entire day will unfold in a positive way too. The positive mind set at the onset of a day plays a huge role in how the individual's day will unfold and how the individual will cope with the events of the day.

Altering Actions

Most people indulge in a daily ritual before embarking on the day ahead. Some of these rituals may include the mind; some may focus on the body, while others would wisely focus on both the body and mind.

Those who are more spiritually in tuned would start the day by addressing this aspect of their life. Preparing the body and mind to reach and remain in a certain spiritual mind set allows the individual the luxury of facing the day with a strong spiritual conviction.

This will then provide the necessary strength and wisdom to work with all the challenges and possible circumstances that are like to unfold during the course of the day.

Others may opt to energize their coming daily activities and schedules with a good physical workout. Exercising regularly and ideally at the beginning of the day allows the body to recharge and revitalize after a good night's rest.

Eating a hearty and healthy meal at the beginning of the day is always advisable. Most medical professional insist that this ritual be practiced without deviation as the first meal is very important in providing the energy for the rest of the day.

Other daily rituals may include having a set routine that is comfortable and less like to cause stress. Planning the day to ensure a smooth flow of activities is always better than running around aimlessly trying to get as many things done as possible. This is a good way to stay motivated as each thing scheduled for the day gets done quickly and effectively.

Chapter 4:

Find Out Your Passions And Them Do That

Synopsis

Working of something that one is passionate about gives the mind and body that extra boost needed to get the task done well and with a feeling of complete satisfaction.

What Do You Love

Discovering the single most important thing at the moment in an individual's life and then working on it to bring it to fruitfulness will require a certain amount of passion to make it a success. But in doing so there is a certain amount of new vitality both in mind and in spirit that bring out the energy and zest required to see the endeavor through.

Keeping as focused as possible is another way to find out what drives an individual. When there are fewer distractions around in the individual's life, the ability to search with a focused mind what the individual is passionate about can be very beneficial.

This focused finding will also increase the chances of the individual embarking on the findings quickly and efficiently because of the level of passion involved.

If the task or endeavor proves to be a difficult one to undertake then the level of passion for the said activity will be what carries the individual to work on it until successful completion is achieved. Being passionate and staying passionate is the deciding factor on the merits of working on the project until completion, therefore this element is a very important ingredient in the make up of success.

Trying many different things may also be one way of actually discovering what the individual is likely to be most passionate about.

However the danger here is that in trying too many different things the individual may end up doing nothing to completion at all. Therefore here again the element of passion plays a huge role in defining what is most enjoyable to the individual.

Chapter 5:

Do For Others

Synopsis

A good motto in life is to do unto others what you would like done unto you. This very real desire has many far reaching connotations. In trying to practice this motto one would be more aware on one's own actions and how it affects others.

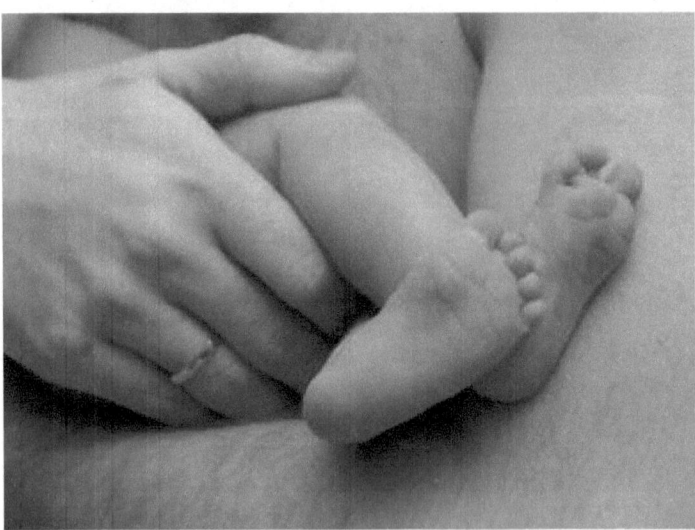

Help

In realizing no man is an island; people acknowledge the fact that in order to have harmony other people's feelings and thoughts must be considered. This will foster better ties between individual and as a group which in turn will create a harmonious and conducive environment.

Daily trying to be more aware of other people's feeling also help an individual to be more sensitive to others and thus be less selfish. This is a good attribute to develop as people generally like being around those who are thoughtful and accommodating.

Always extending a helping hand is also another trait that is rather endearing. More often than not, people who are helpful will always be popular and an asset to have around.

There is also a sense of fulfillment when the hand to help is extended. By doing this it also inculcates the fact that a lot of people will be more than willing to help the individual if the need arises.

Showing a positive side is always a good thing as nobody wants to be unpleasant to someone who is polite, gentle, and giving. These virtues if practiced often enough will eventually reflect back unto the individual and thus cause other to do likewise.

Another popular saying is what goes around comes around is also similar in virtue to the above popular notion. When the example is set to do good those around will learn from this example and try to emulate the wonderful virtue. Thus more people will be more considerate and kind and the world will be a better place indeed.

Chapter 6:

Connect With Nature

Synopsis

Being able to connect with nature has many wonderful benefits both for the good of one's mental health and physical health. Nature is one of God's free gifts to human kind and learning to appreciate it should be everyone's priority. However sadly this is not so, as everyone is busy rushing around trying to keep their lives in order.

Outdoors

Communing with nature will allow a person to slow down and just enjoy what is there for free. It only requires the individual stop and "soak" it all in. spending more time outdoors is one way to connect with nature. Playing or just walking in the park is a healthy way to relax and enjoy each other's company or to just be alone with the beauty offered by nature.

When one is able to consciously connect with nature there will be a significant change in both body and mind. These changes that happen are positive in nature and very beneficial to an individual. Taking the time to really relax and focus on just the pleasure of nature and some quiet time, will allow the body to recharge and yet achieve a certain level of calmness which is gotten from being connected to nature.

All age groups should be taught to stop and connect with nature as often as possible. For kids playing outdoors, taking a nature walk or even working in an environment where they are exposed to animals will help build so many positive attributes in them.

When it comes to teens it may not be as simple. To expect them to spend time with nature can be quite a challenge. However encouraging them to take up an outdoor sport, engaging in seasonal projects that require the outdoor experience or simply learning about the different naturally garnered foods, are just a few ways to entice them to be more connected to nature.

Chapter 7:

Connect With Your Spirituality

Synopsis

Setting aside time everyday to connect with one's spirituality can in most instances be easier said than done. For most people the time set aside to do this may be perceived as wasted and thus the reluctance to do so ends up being detrimental not only to the individual but to all around.

Connect

Connecting spiritually has many benefits both mental and physical. There are several ways an individual can connect with their own spirituality. One of them is through voluntary services. When one sets aside time to become a volunteer, one is actually learning to put another person's needs before one's self. This teachers the individual to be more giving and less selfish.

Spending some alone time everyday communing with the inner spirit is beneficial to both the mental and physical health. Making a conscious effort to let go of all the troubles and cares and simply focus on the potential calmness and serenity that is apparent allows the mind to be able to tackle the problem with renewed strength and vigor.

Practicing sessions of meditation is also a common practice when trying to connect spiritually. Most people seek this style of quite time activity to try and enhance their senses to be able to connect with their inner self.

Praying is also another way to make the ever evasive connection with one's spirituality. If done often and consistently praying can and will be an effective way of ensuring this connection. The peace and calmness one can derive from this will definitely benefit both body and mind.

Spending time with nature will allow one's spiritual senses to be heightened and thus cause the individual to be more sensitive to the surroundings. Through the exercise the body slowly releases its dependence on holding on to any stress and learns to relax thus connecting spiritually.

Chapter 8:

Learn To Forgive Yourself And Others

Synopsis

In order to live a healthy life both mentally and physically one must learn to forgive. Forgiveness allows an individual to work through the hurts and bitterness experienced and to let go of all the negative elements. In embracing the act of forgiveness and moving on the body and mind can then start to experience the peace, hope and joy that is the byproduct of forgiveness.

Forgive

The physical implications are vast and serious when it comes to harboring unforgiveness. There are actual scientific researches that conclusively agree that the body's chemical make up is disturbed dramatically when there is resentment and unforgiveness in the individual.

This disturbance that causes the imbalance will then transcend into either serious or mild unhealthy medical conditions. Some of these conditions can escalate to further seriousness if the unforgiveness goes unchecked.

Perhaps knowing some of the benefits that can be enjoyed if unforgiveness was absent, the individual would be more willing to let go and move on.

Healthier relationships can be fostered when the step to forgive is taken. This is because the individual bearing the grudge will be able to release all the negative energy that is dominant in the unforgiveness element.

A greater level of spiritual and physiological state of well being can be attained. This level of release will also ensure the corresponding peace and joyous feelings to be abounded. Medically, stress levels are considerable lowered as with blood pressures. There will also be less likely symptoms of depression, anxiety, and chronic pains.

Though forgiveness is not an easy thing to do, however it is not only vital bit also possible to achieve. The process of forgiveness starts one step at a time.

It is a committed act of consciously accepting the facts and moving away from the pain and rejections caused. The end desired product is the ability to gain the positive elements of compassion and understanding.

Chapter 9:

Exercise To Release Endorphins

Synopsis

Endorphins – is popularly associated with the exhilaration feelings
brought on by pain, danger, or certain forms of stress.
These endorphins work as sedative receptors to help to suppress pain
or discomfort both in body and mind.

Move Around

A good exercise regiment is also another way to release endorphins. Some athletes are able to push themselves to higher limits because of the release of the endorphins during the exercise regiments. These endorphins dull the pain that would otherwise be felt.

Because these are a natural by product, produced within the human body it is certainly a legal way to getting high and staying that way for a period of time. Also to date there are no known negative side effects to the production of endorphins in the human body makeup.

A lot of people advocate turning to an exercise regimen that can be quite exhausting in order to produce the relevant levels of endorphins to suppress the presence of any negative feelings or physical pain. The adequate release of endorphins can ensure the individual stays in a state of bliss.

Some medical experts are at odds as to whether the endorphins are released by the physical exercise or because of the mental pressure from meeting the physical challenge. However all agree that exercising is a great way to release the endorphin levels into the body system.

It should be noted that endorphins are not only released through an exercise regiment but can be released through other activities too. These may include eating spicy food or achieving an orgasm during a

sexual act. Both very different scenarios but both are capable of producing the same amounts of endorphins to create a state of pleasure. Thus the practice of seeking some level of pleasure through the release of endorphin is pretty common as it does not require unusual or difficult processes.

Chapter 10:

How Your Sadness Can Affect Others

Synopsis

Seeking help to address this state of constant sadness is necessary, otherwise there may come a time when the individual has no friends around who are willing to stand by him or her.

Some Hints

When it comes to family members, having to live with someone who is in a constant state of sadness is very challenging indeed. The guilt that the family members feel can cause further negative energy to be expounded. Family member may also feel guilty for any happiness that have or are able to achieve when faced with the individual's sadness. There is also the danger of anger feelings manifesting within the family unit if the individual suffering from sadness is unwilling to seek the necessary help to address the problem.

Friend will also slowly turn away from the individual if there is a constant aura of sadness around the individual. Here also the general feeling of happiness can cause everyone to feel suppressed for fear of offending the individual going through the sadness stage. If continued unchecked this general resentment can snowball into causing others to be unsympathetic toward the individual going through the sadness stage.

An even more negative result of constantly being sad is the health issues that it can cause. When these health issues become severe, the others around who may initially try to be supportive will eventually lose whatever patience they have for the individual going through the sadness phase.

Wrapping Up

Generally people like being around other happy people, thus when one is constantly sad or down there is a very real possibility that the percentage of people willing to be around are almost nil. There is already a lot of stress and strife in the world so adding to it by being in a constant state of sadness will not only be damaging but is also quite unhealthy.

www.ingramcontent.com/pod-product-compliance
Lightning Source LLC
Chambersburg PA
CBHW021417170526
45164CB00002B/687